THE ADOPTION MOVEMENT

SAVING SOULS

A SIMPLE WAY TO SAVE YOU AND YOUR NEIGHBOR'S SOUL THROUGH JESUS CHRIST

Esmeralda Kiczek

2012 by Esmeralda Kiczek

Nihil obstat: Rev. Msgr. James M. Cafone, S.T.D.
Imprimatur: Most Rev. John J. Meyers, D.D., J.C.D.,
Archbishop of Newark

Published by
Bezalel Books
Waterford, MI
www.BezalelBooks.com

The choicest first fruits of your soil
you shall bring to the house of the Lord, your God.
~Exodus 23:19

Printed in the United States of America

Scripture quotes taken from:

The New American Bible by World Catholic Press

Douay Rheims Catholic Bible. http://www.drbo.org/ (online)

ISBN 978-1-936453-02-3
Library of Congress Control Number 2012932182

Cover Art Work by Kuni Strange

THE ADOPTION MOVEMENT

SAVING SOULS

Our Lord told Saint Mechtilde, "If any one out of pure Love of God prays for another person as though he was praying for himself, his prayer shall enlighten the heavenly Jerusalem like the morning sun."

From Devotion for the Dying
By Ven. Mother Mary Potter 22-23

This book is dedicated to all the readers of this book, who I solemnly promised to adopt as my spiritual brothers and sisters. I promise you to pray for the salvation of your soul and that of your dear families for the rest of my life and into eternity.

Your sister in Christ,
Esmeralda Kiczek

THE ADOPTION MOVEMENT

SAVING SOULS

Table of Contents

Chapter 1

SEEK FIRST THE KINGDOM OF GOD

"Seek ye therefore first the kingdom of God, and his justice, and all these things shall be added unto you" (Matthew 6:33).

"This is the generation of them that seek Him, of them that seek the face of the God of Jacob" (Psalms 23:6). We are the generation that seeks the face of our Savior, Jesus Christ. We were created for no other reason, but for us to do the will of Our Father in Heaven. In order for us to truly do the will of Our Father, we must seek Him first above all things. He who gave up His only Son, Jesus, for us sinners, wants us to seek Him first. Let us listen to His call. When Jesus laid down His precious life for us, He put us first and His life last, He did not think twice to lay down His life for us. Now, He is asking us to put Him first, to seek Him first. Let us not be afraid to do the Will of God because He is Love and Mercy Itself. "Therefore, if you be risen with Christ, seek the things that are above; where Christ is sitting at the right hand of God" (Colossians 3:1). If we do this, everything else will be given to us.

" 'Our bread': The Father who gives us life cannot but give us the nourishment life requires — all appropriate goods and blessings, both material and spiritual. In the Sermon on the Mount, Jesus insists on the filial trust that cooperates with our Father's providence. He is not inviting us to idleness, but wants to relieve us from nagging worry and preoccupation. Such is the filial surrender of the children of God" (Catechism 2830). Our Father has promised to give us everything if we seek Him first. It is that simple my brothers and sisters, seek God first with all of your hearts and He alone will provide for everything we need. "To those who seek the kingdom of God and his righteousness, He has promised to give all else besides. Since everything indeed belongs to God, he who possesses God wants for nothing, if he himself is not found wanting before God" (Catechism 2830).

On the other hand, if we seek this world first and not God we will be in danger of not inheriting the Kingdom of God. "The Lord grieves over the rich, because they find their consolation in the abundance of goods. 'Let the proud seek and love earthly kingdoms, but blessed are the poor in spirit for theirs is the Kingdom of heaven.' Abandonment to the providence of the Father in heaven frees us from anxiety about tomorrow. Trust in God is a preparation for the blessedness of the poor. They shall see God" (Catechism 2547). This is the solution my dear brothers and sisters to our life's problems and the constant worries that consume our lives every day, "Abandonment to the providence of God." Why should we fear to abandon ourselves entirely to Our Creator who loves us so much that He gave His only Son for us. We are God's children, He is Our Father, let us trust Him with all of our hearts and He will take care of all of our needs. Trust is the key. We must trust Him. If you do not know how to trust Him, ask Him to give you the grace to trust Him and to love Him as He deserves. He will give it to you, as He has said, "Amen, amen I say to you, if you ask the Father any thing in My Name, He will give it to you" (John 16:23). These are the words of Jesus, so you must trust Him. Ask for the graces necessary for us to seek Him always. He needs to be our first priority in our lives.

My brothers and sisters what do you have to lose, start today to do the Will of Our Father in heaven who loves you more than His life, seek Him first above all things and everything else will be provided for you. "With creation, God does not abandon His creatures to themselves. He not only gives them being and existence, but also, and at every moment, upholds and sustains them in being, enables them to act and brings them to their final end. Recognizing this utter dependence with respect to the Creator is a source of wisdom and freedom, of joy and confidence" (Catechism 301). "Jesus asks for childlike abandonment to the providence of our heavenly Father who takes care of his children's smallest needs: Therefore do not be anxious, saying, 'What shall we eat?' or 'What shall we drink?' ... Your heavenly Father knows that you need them all. But seek first his kingdom and his righteousness, and all these things shall be yours as well" (Catechism 305).

My brothers and sisters, seeking God and our salvation do not end at the time of our conversions, but continues throughout our lives. We must try to get to know and love God each day more and more. We need to ask for all the graces necessary for our state in life, to love with all of our heart, soul, mind, and strength. We must do the Will of Our

Father in Heaven. He wills for all of us to be saved. We need to acquire a hatred for sin. We need to pray for the graces necessary to avoid sin. We need to use the sacrament of reconciliation often. We must desire to please God in every way we can. We need to strive to enhance daily our personal relationship with the living God (Father, Jesus, Holy Spirit) this is the absolute most important thing we can do, everything else is secondary. "Seek the LORD while he may be found; call on him while he is near" (Isaiah 55:6). Do we realize that we actually have a command to seek God? To seek God must be our most glorious and rewarding assignment in our lives. The primary purpose God allows any of us to be born here on earth is to please and glorify Him. We can please and glorify Our Lord by helping our brothers and sisters obtain the graces necessary through Jesus to save their souls and ours by prayer and sacrifice. God makes some promises to those who seek him. The Bible says, "Blessed are those who hunger and thirst for righteousness, for they will be satisfied" (Matthew 5:6). We read that those who seek God will not lack (Psalm 34:10); and that they will rejoice (1 Chronicles 16:10). Let us do everything with God, for God and in God.

We are also assured that seekers will find. God says, "Ask, and it will be given you; seek and you will find; knock and the door will be opened to you" (Matthew 7:7). We are encouraged to seek the Lord like we would seek great treasure; "And if you look for it as for silver and search for it as for hidden treasure, then you will understand the fear of the LORD and find the Knowledge of God" (Proverbs 2:4-5). Perhaps best of all, God promises a revival for those who seek Him. He says, "And my people, upon whom My Name has been pronounced, humble themselves and pray, and seek my presence and turn from their evil ways, I will hear from heaven and pardon their sins and revive their land" (2 Chronicles 7:14). Let us humble ourselves and ask for forgiveness for all of our brothers and sisters as well as for ourselves and pray for each others' soul. Trust in Him because everything is possible if we believe in Him. It is that simple, my brothers and sisters, the first thing we must do in order to save our souls and to help our neighbors to obtain the graces to save their soul through Jesus is to seek God above all things.

Let us start to do the Will of Our Father in Heaven and start to work for the Kingdom of God. "He saith to his disciples, the harvest indeed is great, but the laborers are few" (Matthew 9:37). "Do not store up for yourselves treasures on earth, where moth and decay destroys and thieves break in and steal. But store up treasures in heaven, where neither moth nor decay destroy, nor thieves break in and steal. For where your treasure is, there also will your heart be. The lamp of the body is the eye. If your eye is sound, your whole body will be filled with light; but if your eye is bad, your whole body will be in darkness. And if the light in you is darkness, how great will the darkness be. No one can serve two masters. He will either hate one and love the other, or be devoted to the one and despise the other. You cannot serve God and mammon. Therefore I tell you, do not worry about your life, what you will eat [or drink], or about your body, what you will wear. Is not life more than food and the body more than clothing? Look at the birds in the sky; they do not sow or reap, they gather nothing into barns, yet your heavenly Father feeds them. Are not you more important than they? Can any of you by worrying add a single moment to your life span? Why

11

are you anxious about clothes? Learn from the way the wild flowers grow. They do not work or spin. But I tell you that not even Solomon in all his splendor was clothed like one of them. If God so clothes the grass of the field, which grows today and is thrown into the oven tomorrow, will he not much more provide for you, O you of little faith? So do not worry and say, 'What are we to eat?' or 'What are we to drink?' or 'What are we to wear?' All these things the pagans seek. Your heavenly Father knows that you need them all. But seek first the kingdom [of God] and his righteousness, and all these things will be given you besides. Do not worry about tomorrow; tomorrow will take care of itself. Sufficient for a day is its own evil" (Matthew 6:19-34). We cannot by being anxious add a single hour to our life span.

We need to have childlike trust in Our Father because it is pleasing to God. He wants to give us everything, but the key to obtain everything from God is to do His Will above all things and we must trust Him, otherwise, we tie His hands and He can't help us. "'Give us:' The trust of children who look to their Father for everything is beautiful. 'He makes his sun rise on the evil and on the good, and sends rain on the just and on the unjust.' He gives to all the living 'their food in due season.' Jesus teaches us this petition, because it glorifies our Father by acknowledging how good he is, beyond all goodness"(Catechism 2828). Give yourselves entirely to God and He will in exchange bestow on you everything you need without reserve. My brothers and sisters give glory to Our Heavenly Father by seeking Him first always in all things and at all times without reserve and He will take care of you. He loves you, you are precious to Him. So, my brothers and sisters the first thing one must do in order to get the graces to help save our soul and our neighbor's soul is to seek first the kingdom of God and Our Lord will take care of everything thing else we need. We must trust in His words. Always remember this: "Heaven and earth will pass away, but My words will not pass away" (Matthew 24:35).

The Adoption Movement: Saving Souls

Chapter 2

LOVE OF GOD AND LOVE OF NEIGHBOR

"Jesus said to him: Thou shalt love the Lord thy God with thy whole heart, and with thy whole soul, and with thy whole mind. This is the greatest and the first commandment. And the second is like to this: Thou shalt love thy neighbor as thyself" (Matthew 22:37-39).

"If I speak in human and angelic tongues but do not have love, I am a resounding gong or a clashing cymbal. And if I have the gift of prophecy and comprehend all mysteries and all knowledge; if I have all faith so as to move mountains but do not have love, I am nothing. If I give away everything I own, and if I hand my body over so that I may boast but do not have love, I gain nothing. Love is patient, love is kind. It is not jealous, (love) is not pompous, it is not inflated, it is not rude, it does not seek its own interests, it is not quick-tempered, it does not brood over injury, it does not rejoice over wrongdoing but rejoices with the truth. It bears all things, believes all things, hopes all things, and endures all things. Love never fails. If there are prophecies, they will be brought to nothing; if tongues, they will cease; if knowledge, it will be brought to nothing. For we know partially and we prophesy partially, but when the perfect comes, the partial will pass away. When I was child, I used to talk as a child, think as a child, reason as a child; when I became a man, I put aside childish things. At present we see indistinctly, as in a mirror, but then face to face. At present I know partially; then I shall know fully, as I am fully known. So faith, hope, love remain, these three; but the greatest of these is love" (1 Corinthians 13:1-13). As St. Catherine of Siena said, "Everything comes from love, all is ordained for the salvation of man, God does nothing without this goal in mind." Love is the greatest gift from God. Love is the only thing that is eternal. If we truly have love for Our Creator and love for our brothers and sisters, then we have everything. Love is the characteristic by which a Christian should be known above all else.

The first commandment that Our Lord Jesus gave us is: "You shall love the Lord your God with all your heart, with all your soul, with all your mind, and with all your strength" (Mark 12:30). And the second commandment is: "You shall love your neighbor as yourself. There is no other commandments greater than these" (Mark 12:31). These are the two greatest commandments that we must follow in order for us to inherit the kingdom of God. It is very simple, love God and love your neighbor. "The Ten Commandments state what is required in the love of God and love of neighbor. The first three concern love of God, and the other seven, love of neighbor. As charity comprises the two commandments to which the Lord related the whole Law and the prophets ... so the Ten Commandments were themselves given on two tablets. Three were written on one tablet and seven on the other. (Catechism 2067).

The Catechism says, "God created everything for man, but man in turn was created to serve and love God and to offer all creation back to him: What is it that is about to be created, that enjoys such honor? It is man that great and wonderful living creature, more precious in the eyes of God than all other creatures! For him the heavens and the earth, the sea and all the rest of creation exist. God attached so much importance to his salvation that He did not spare His own Son for the sake of man. Nor does He ever cease to work, trying every possible means, until He has raised man up to Himself and made him sit at His right hand" (Catechism 358). He loves you so much and He thirsts for the salvation of all.

"The Word became flesh so that thus we might know God's love: 'In this the love of God was made manifest among us, that God sent his only Son into the world, so that we might live through him.' 'For God so loved the world that He gave His only Son, that whoever believes in Him should not perish but have eternal life'" (Catechism 458). God gave up His only Son for you and for me. Let us return this love to Our Heavenly Father by loving Him with all of hearts, souls, minds, and strength above all.

Let us pray as St. John Vianney did, "I love you, O my God, and my only desire is to love you until the last breath of my life. I love you, O my infinitely lovable God, and I would rather die loving you, than live without loving you. I love you, Lord, and the only grace I ask is to love you eternally. ... My God, if my tongue cannot say in every moment that I love you, I want my heart to repeat it to you as often as I draw breath" (Catechism 2658).

"'God is Love' and love is his first gift, containing all others. 'God's love has been poured into our hearts through the Holy Spirit who has been given to us'" (Catechism 733).

So, my brothers and sisters let us keep Him in our hearts at all times. He wants to take rest in our hearts.

How can we show God how much we love Him? One way we can show God that we love Him is by helping Jesus do what He loves the most, to save souls. We can help our brothers and sisters to obtain the graces necessary for their healing, conversion and salvation by offering our prayers and sacrifices through Jesus Christ to Our Heavenly Father. Jesus poured out all his blood on the cross for all souls of mankind. Our Lord Jesus told Saint Faustina, "I thirst. I thirst for the salvation of souls. Help me, my daughter, to save souls. Join your sufferings to My Passion and offer them to the heavenly Father for sinners" (Diary of St. Faustina, 1032). Our Lord is asking you and me to help Him save His dear children by offering all of your sufferings and united to the Passion of Jesus for the souls of our brothers and sisters. We encounter many burdens every day, we must not waste them, and we should use them to obtain the graces for the healing, conversion, and salvation of our brothers and sisters. It is up to you to listen to the call of your Redeemer, who is saying to you, "Help Me My son/daughter to save souls." Is there anything more important than the work of helping our brothers and sisters save their souls through Jesus?

" 'Our Father' desires all men to be saved and to come to the knowledge of the truth. He 'is forbearing toward you, not wishing that any should perish.' His commandment is 'that you love one another; even as I have loved you, that you also love one another.' This commandment summarizes all the others and expresses His entire will" (Catechism 2822). This is the will for you and me, my brothers and sisters, to love God and to love our neighbor for the glory of Our Heavenly Father.

The apostle St. Paul reminds us of this: "He who loves his neighbor has fulfilled the law. The commandments, 'You shall not commit adultery, you shall not kill, you shall not steal, you shall not covet,' and any other commandment, are summed up in this sentence, 'You shall love your neighbor as yourself.' Love does no wrong to a neighbor; therefore love is the fulfilling of the law" (Catechism 2196).

How can we love our neighbor?

There is no better way than to help our brothers and sisters obtain the graces to save their souls through the One who gave up His life for them, Our Lord Jesus. For you could do everything for them but if they are lost to the fires of hell of what did all the work help them? This is what the Gospel of Matthew, chapter 6, verse 19 says that we should "lay up treasures in heaven where neither moth nor rust can destroy," the treasures are the souls of our brothers and sisters. What can be more precious than the souls of our brothers and sisters? Who would not want to help save an immortal soul from the eternal misery of the loss of God? This is true love of neighbor, help them save their souls by uniting our prayers and sacrifices to the sufferings of Jesus. When we unite our suffering to those of Jesus, they will bear much fruit because He is Our Savior. If we truly love God with our whole heart, with our whole soul, with our whole mind, and with whole strength, then we will also love our neighbor as ourselves. My brothers and sisters the love that you have for your Father in Heaven and the love you have for your neighbor will give great glory to Our Heavenly Father. Let us Glorify Him always.

"Could you say you loved your neighbor as yourself if you saw him dying alone, uncared for, and did not assist him? Could you see him most cruelly slaughtered without an attempt to save him? All over the world souls are dying, are perishing, falling into the bottomless abyss from which there is no redemption. Before it is too late, will you not raise one cry to Heaven for mercy, before the final sentence is pronounced, before the awful words, "Depart from Me you cursed," have been spoken to that then most miserable soul?" (Devotion for the Dying by Ven. Mother Mary Potter p 118).

There is nothing more important on earth for a person to do other than help save souls as well as his own through our Lord Jesus Christ. The Apostle James said through the Holy Spirit, "Whoever brings back a sinner will save his soul from death and will cover a multitude of sins" (James 5:20). My dear brothers and sisters you are not only helping your neighbors save their souls by bringing their souls to Jesus through prayer and sacrifice but at the same time you are saving yours. Think about it. This is truly love of God and neighbor. It is that simple my brothers and sisters, Jesus thirsts while on the Cross for the salvation of every human soul. Let us help Him quench His thirst by offering our prayers and sacrifices for the souls of our brothers and sisters in order to help them save their soul. Everything else is secondary, so it is up to you to choose, but remember there are only two roads, hell or heaven, those are the only choices we have. But if you choose to fulfill the law of the two commandments, to love God and to love your neighbor as yourself, you will be on the right path that will eventually lead to your Father in Heaven.

"God has purposely left to you a part of the work of saving souls. It is to His Glory that you should imitate His Son, in whom He is well pleased, that you should become like to Jesus, that you should do the work He did, that you should be filled with His love for souls that you should be ready to lay down your life for them. Jesus does not require that you should die for them, but rather you should live for them and offer to the Eternal Father His own Passion, His own Holy Life and Death, which He has put into your hands to do with as you please. Jesus has given you this power, that by your cooperation with Him in the saving of souls you may the more resemble Him, and that He may live again in His Members and that God, looking from Heaven may see upon this earth living copies of Jesus, Jesus multiplied in His Members and thus more pleasing will this earth appear to Him then when in the beginning He looked upon it and was pleased and pronounced it good" (Devotion for the Dying by Ven. Mother Mary Potter pp118-119). My brothers and sisters, we need to offer to the Eternal Father our prayers and sacrifices in union with the sufferings of Jesus for the salvation of souls because it is only through Him that we all can be saved. As Jesus said, "I am the gate. Whoever enters through Me, will be saved, and will come in and go out and find pasture ... I came that they may have life, and have it more abundantly" (John 10:9-10). Jesus has shown us the way to obtain the graces for the healing, conversion and salvation of our brothers and sisters, and it is only through Jesus Christ that we can be saved. As St. Frances Xavier Cabrini said, "We must pray without tiring, for the salvation of mankind does not depend upon material success but on Jesus alone."

Let us join together my brothers and sisters with all of our hearts to the prayer of Saint Augustine who said to his flock, "I desire not to be saved without you." Our flock is our brothers and sisters all around us; let us help them save their souls through Jesus for the glory of God, the Father.

Chapter 3

THE DIVINE MERCY OF GOD

"Praise ye the God of gods: for his mercy endureth for ever"
(Psalms 135:2).

My brothers and sisters the greatest attribute of God is Mercy. He is LOVE and Mercy itself. We resemble God most when we forgive our brothers and sisters. We must forgive them in order for us to obtain mercy from God. Jesus said to St. Faustina, "Every soul, and especially the soul of every religious, should reflect my mercy. My heart overflows with compassion and mercy for all. The heart of my beloved must resemble mine; from her heart must spring the fountain of My mercy for souls; otherwise I will not acknowledge her as Mine" (Diary of St. Faustina, 1148). "Proclaim that mercy is the greatest attribute of God" (Diary of St. Faustina, 301). God is calling us to show mercy for our brothers and sisters who are in danger of losing their souls to the fires of hell. We must show mercy otherwise Jesus said that He will not acknowledge us as His. A very simple way for us to show mercy is to help our brothers and sisters save their souls by praying and offering sacrifices for them through the Passion and Death of Our Lord Jesus Christ. "Blessed are the merciful, for they shall obtain mercy" (One of the Beatitudes). We all need the mercy of Our Father in Heaven. Please Dear God, have mercy on all of your children. Amen.

Jesus said to St. Faustina, "My love and mercy knows no bounds" (Diary of St. Faustina, 718). How beautiful it is to know that Our Father is willing to show us mercy as many times as we need it. He is The Father of Mercy and Love. My brothers and sisters, we can draw the graces of God's mercy only with one vessel and one vessel only and that is trust. We must trust Jesus if we want to obtain mercy from Him. Jesus said to St. Faustina, "The more a soul trusts, the more it will receive. Souls that trust boundlessly are a great comfort to Me, because I pour all the treasures of My graces into them. I rejoice that they ask for much, because it is My desire to give much, very much. On the other hand, I am sad when souls ask for little, when they narrow their hearts" (Diary of St. Faustina, 1578). The Lord made it clear to St. Faustina that the more we trust in Him and strive to live His will and not ours, the more graces we will receive. He told her "Tell [all people], My daughter, that I am Love and Mercy itself. When a soul approaches Me with trust, I fill it with such an abundance of graces that it cannot contain them within itself, but radiates them to other souls" (Diary of St. Faustina 1074). So, trust is the key to obtain God's mercy for ourselves and for others. So, let us be confident and trust in God with all our hearts when we pray through Jesus for the healing, conversion, and salvation of our brothers and sisters. He desires to give us much, so let us ask for much.

Jesus longs for souls — He longs for the conversion of sinners. The greatest sinners have the most right to His mercy. He comes first. "Let the greatest sinners place their trust in My mercy. They have the right before others to trust in the abyss of My mercy" (Diary of St. Faustina, 1146). No matter how great the sin, God's Mercy is ALWAYS greater. Let us not be afraid to approach Our Lord because of our sins. He said that His Mercy and love is always greater than any of our sins.

"Justification is the most excellent work of God's love made manifest in Christ Jesus and granted by the Holy Spirit. It is the opinion of St. Augustine that 'the justification of the wicked is a greater work than the creation of heaven and earth,' because 'heaven and earth will pass away but the salvation and justification of the elect ... will not pass away' He holds also that the justification of sinners surpasses the creation of the angels in justice, in that it bears witness to a greater mercy" (Catechism 1994).

Jesus said to St. Faustina, "I desire that you know more profoundly the love that burns in My Heart for souls, and you will understand this when you meditate upon My Passion. Call upon My mercy on behalf of sinners; I desire their salvation. When you say this prayer, with a contrite heart and with faith on behalf of some sinner, I will give him the grace of conversion. This is the prayer: O Blood and Water, which gushed forth from the Heart of Jesus as a fount of Mercy for us, I trust in You" (Diary of St. Faustina, 186-87). With this simple prayer we can obtain the conversions of many sinners. Let us, pray this prayer often with a contrite heart and faith in God who desires the salvation of all our souls. This is a simple way to help save souls. Do not neglect to pray for our brothers and sisters who are in danger of losing their souls to the flames of hell.

The Lord also said to St. Faustina, "The loss of each soul plunges Me into mortal sadness. You always console Me when you pray for sinners. The prayer most pleasing to Me is prayer for the conversion of sinners. Know, My daughter, that this prayer is always heard and answered" (Diary of St. Faustina, 1397). Let us not allow Our Lord and Savior to ever be mortally sad again because of the loss of a beloved son or daughter of His to the fires of hell. So, let us storm heaven with prayers and sacrifices for the healing, conversion, and salvation of our brothers and sisters.

My brothers and sisters, Our Lord Jesus makes great promises to those who spread this devotion and trust in Him. "But God has promised a great grace especially to all those ... who will proclaim My great mercy. I shall protect them Myself at the hour of death, as My own glory. And even if the sins of soul are as dark as night, when the sinner turns to My mercy he gives Me the greatest praise and is the glory of My Passion. When a soul praises My goodness, Satan trembles before it and flees to the very bottom of hell" (Diary of St. Faustina, 378).

Our Lord is told St. Faustina that He will attend to the sanctification of our souls if we adore His mercy and have great trust in Him. "Let souls who are striving for perfection particularly adore My mercy, because the abundance of graces which I grant them flows from My mercy. I desire that these souls distinguish themselves by boundless trust in My mercy. I Myself will attend to the sanctification of such souls. I will provide them with everything they will need to attain sanctity" (Diary of St. Faustina, 1578). We must distinguish ourselves by the great trust in Jesus' mercy. It is simple: adore His mercy and trust Him with all your heart in order for your soul to attain sanctity as Jesus promised that He Himself will help us. "So let us then with confidently approach the throne of grace to receive mercy and find grace for timely help" (Hebrews 4:16). This is the time in need, today more than ever we need the mercy of Our Lord to help all of us, especially to save our souls and those of our neighbors. "Keep yourselves in the love of God, waiting for the mercy of our Lord Jesus Christ, unto life everlasting" (Jude 1:21). The mercy of our God will come, my dear brothers and sisters and we will all get to see it if we adore and trust in His mercy.

Jesus asked St. Faustina to "Fight for the salvation of souls, exhorting them to trust in My mercy, as that is your task in this life and in the life to come" (Diary of St. Faustina 1452). So, let this be our task also to fight for the souls of our brothers and sisters by helping them to trust in the Mercy of God.

Chapter 4

PRAYER

"But we will give ourselves continually to prayer, and to the ministry of the word" (Acts of Apostles 6:4).

Jesus said, "This is how you are to pray: Our Father in heaven, hallowed be your name, your kingdom come, your will be done, on earth as in heaven. Give us today our daily bread; and forgive us our debts, as we forgive our debtors; and do not subject us to the final test, but deliver us from the evil one.

When we call God, **Our Father**, we acknowledge that we are all brothers and sisters through Jesus and we have the same Father in Heaven.

Hallowed be thy Name — we should glorify God's name at all times and the best way to do this is to bring souls to the Father.

Thy Kingdom Come — The Kingdom is souls that love God, let God's Kingdom reign over all souls. Seek the Kingdom of God first and God will provide for everything else we need.

Thy Will be Done — "God wills everyone to be saved" (1 Timothy 2-4). So we should pray this with great desire for the salvation of our brothers and sisters.

On Earth as it is in Heaven — What a beautiful world it will be when we all love God and our neighbor as ourselves. It would be heaven on earth.

Give us this day our daily bread — With seeking God first, all our other needs will be satisfied in this world and in the next.

And forgive us our trespasses as we forgive those who trespass against us — Not only should we forgive them we should pray for their salvation. Jesus said, "But I say to you, Love your enemies: do good to them that hate you: and pray for them that persecute and calumniate you" (Matthew 5:44).

And lead us not into temptation, but deliver us from evil, amen — We all need God's help and grace so judge not your brothers and sisters, pray for them that God will give them the grace to be led out of temptation and deliver them from the evil one. We are weak and without prayers could fall. Amen, Praise the Lord.

Let us learn, "from this prayer of the 'Our Father,' how pleasing it must be to God to pray for others. In this prayer Jesus Christ teaches us to not only pray for ourselves, but also for all our fellow men. He also taught us, by His example to pray for others. Indeed, we may say that His whole life was a continual prayer for the just, as well as for sinners"(*Prayer The Key to Salvation* pp.106).

Our Lord's desire that we should pray for one another is shown plainly in the revelations made to Saint Mechtilde, Jesus said, "If anyone out of pure love of God prays for another person as though he was praying for himself, his prayer shall enlighten the heavenly Jerusalem like the morning sun." We need to pray for our brothers and sisters as if we were praying for ourselves and we will "enlighten the heavenly Jerusalem like the morning sun." Prayer is a great gift from Our Father in Heaven; let us use this wonderful gift for obtaining the graces through the merits of His Holy Passion for the salvation of our dear brothers and sisters for the Glory of Our Lord and Savior.

"Necessity obliges us to pray for ourselves but charity must induce us to pray for others. The prayer of fraternal charity is more acceptable to God than that of necessity. The prayer for sinners, says St. Alphonsus, is not only beneficial to them, but is, moreover, most pleasing to God; and the Lord Himself complains of His servants who do not recommend sinners to Him" (*Prayer The Key to Salvation* pp.107-108). My brothers and sisters open your hearts to fraternal charity and love for your neighbors and pray for their healing, conversion, and salvation.

"Souls," says St. Alphonsus, "that really love God, will never neglect to pray for poor sinners." Right now you have the opportunity to show God that you really love Him by interceding through prayer for the souls of your brothers and sisters.

"Confess therefore your sins one to another: and pray one for another, that you may be saved. For the continual prayer of a just man availeth much" (James 5:16). When

31

Moses interceded for the Israelites when Our Lord wanted to wiped them off the face of the earth because they had fallen into idol worship even after all He had done for them. God said to Moses. "Let me alone that my wrath may be enkindled against them, and that I may destroy them" (Exodus 32:10). "Behold the struggle between an angry God and His suppliant servant; between justice and prayer. 'Let Me alone,' said the Lord, 'Let Me destroy this ungrateful people and I will make thee the leader of a great nation.' Now as Saint Jerome remarks, 'He who says to another; let me alone evidently shows that he is subject to the power of another.' But Moses would not yield; on the contrary, he confidently entreated the Lord to pardon the Jews: 'Why O Lord,' he asked, 'is Thy indignation aroused against Thy People who Thou has brought out of the Land of Egypt with great power and with a mighty hand? Let not the Egyptians boast I beseech Thee; he craftily brought them out, that he might kill them in the mountains and efface them from the earth: let Thy anger cease, and be appeased upon the waywardness of Thy people' (Exodus 32:11-12). Now what was the issue of this struggle between the justice of God and the confident prayer of Moses; for 'the Lord was appeased,' says Holy Scripture, 'and did not the evil which had spoken against his people'"(Exodus 32:14, *Prayer The Key to Salvation* pp.76). Let us become like Moses and intercede for our brothers and sisters who are in great need of our prayers in order to help them obtain the graces for their healing, conversion, and salvation.

"The prayer of the just man, "says St. Augustine," is a key to heaven; let his prayer ascend to heaven and God's Mercy will descend on earth."(*Prayer The Key to Salvation* pp.80). Let us pray for God's mercy to fall upon our brothers and sisters so that we all may be saved. For Jesus has said, "Ask and it shall be given you: seek, and you shall find: knock and it shall be opened to you" (Matthew 7:7). Let us ask, seek and knock with confidence for the graces necessary for the healing, conversion and salvation of our brothers and sisters. Jesus also said, "Amen, amen I say to you whatsoever you ask my Father in my name, He will give it you." The word, 'Amen, Amen,' is equivalent in the Hebrew language to a solemn oath. Who knowing that God has promised so solemnly to hear our prayers can still harbor the least doubt when he prays in the Name of Jesus Christ? Who does not see that such want of confidence would be a great offense against the Omnipotence, Goodness, and Fidelity of God? No! God, who is infinite Holiness, Justice Itself, cannot deceive us; He will not make a promise unless He intends to fulfill it.'(*Prayer The Key to Salvation* pp.160). Know that our prayers for the conversion and salvation of our brothers and sisters will always be heard and answered. Jesus Christ has made this promise, and He will never fail to keep it. . "Amen, I say to you, until heaven and earth pass away, not the smallest part of the letter will pass from the law, until all things have taken place" (Matthew 5:18).

Our Lord Jesus told St. Faustina, "The prayer most pleasing to Me is the prayer for conversion of sinners. Know my daughter, that this prayer is always heard and answered" (Diary of St. Faustina 1397). "And we have this confidence in Him, that if we ask anything according to His will, He hears us. And if we know that He hears us in regard to whatever we ask, we know that what we have asked Him for is ours" (1 John 5:14-15). This is a promise from Jesus, so know that when you pray for the conversion of your brothers and sisters, Jesus will answer your prayer.

Jesus wants souls, He died for them, and that is the sole purpose of our religion and Church. If we pray for the conversion of sinners, you will be helping God make great saints for the greatest sinners become the greatest saints and the greatest imitators of Jesus, by their love and zeal in the work of saving souls. St. Paul is a perfect example of this because St. Stephen prayed for St. Paul's conversion.

"Consider the efficacy of prayer. We have only to pray for lawful things, to pray for them often and perseveringly, and to believe we shall receive them, and receive them too, not according to the poverty of our poor intentions, but according to the riches, wisdom, and munificence of God, and it is an infallible truth that we shall receive them" (*Devotion to the Dying* by Ven. Mother Mary Potter pp. 123).

God wants us to pray for everyone because God wants to save everyone. "This is good and pleasing to God our Savior, who wills everyone to be saved and to come to knowledge of the truth" (1 Timothy 2:3-4). St. Paul says: "First of all, then, I ask that supplications, prayers, petitions, and thanksgivings be offered for everyone" (1 Timothy 2:1). Let us not waste any time and start today to pray for our brothers and sisters. St. Therese of Lisieux said, "We have only short moments of this life to work for God's glory. The devil knows this and that is why he tries to make us waste time in useless things. O, let us not waste our time! Let us save souls! Souls are falling into hell innumerable as the flakes of snow on a winter day. Jesus weeps! Instead of consoling Him we are brooding over our own sorrows ... There is only one thing to do during the brief day, or rather, night of this life: Love Jesus with all the strength of your heart and save souls for Him, so that He may be loved!"

"By prayer we can discern 'what is the will of God' and obtain the endurance to do it. Jesus teaches us that one enters the kingdom of heaven not by speaking words, but by doing the will of my Father in heaven" (Catechism 2826). God wills the salvation of everyone, "For God so loved the world that He gave His only son, so that everyone who believes in Him might not perish but might have eternal life" (John 3:16).

As Fr. Mueller said in the book, *Prayer the Key to Salvation*, page 32, "He alone is lost who does not pray; he alone will be saved who perseveres in prayer. On the Last Day, all the saints of Heaven, as well as also all the dammed souls of Hell, will bear witness to this truth; on that great day you, too, will bear witness to it, either with the elect on the right, if you have prayed during life, or with the dammed on the left, if you have neglected to pray. Choose now whichever lot you prefer, but choose in time" And remember, "He must know that he who causeth a sinner to be converted from the error of his way, shall save his soul from death, and shall cover a multitude of sins" (James 5:20). We are not only helping our brothers and sisters to save their souls but we are also helping ourselves to be saved through the Passion and Death of Jesus.

"God gives to all this wonderful gift of prayer, all can pray, rich and poor, the learned and the ignorant, the old and the young. God is at our disposal. He allow us this almost unbounded influence over Him" (*Devotion to the Dying* by Ven. Mother Mary Potter pp. 123-124). He waits for our prayers, so that He can answer them. He always hears us when we pray.

Know this my dear brothers and sisters that, "There is nothing more holy in this world than to work for the good of souls, for whose salvation Jesus Christ poured out the last drops of His Blood" (St. John Bosco). Let us join in this great battle and offer all our prayers for the healing, conversion, and salvation of our brothers and sisters.

Chapter 5

SACRIFICES

"But for what glory is it, if committing sin, and being buffeted for it, you endure? But if doing well you suffer patiently; this is thankworthy before God. For unto this are called: because Christ also suffered for us, leaving you an example that you should follow his steps"
(1 Peter 2:20-22).

"Let us run by patience to the fight proposed to us: looking on Jesus, the author and finisher of faith, who having joy set before Him, endured the Cross, despising the shame, and now seated on the right hand of the throne of God. Think diligently upon Him that endured such opposition from sinners against Himself; that you be not wearied, fainting in your minds" (Hebrews 12:1-3). Be brave, my dear brothers and sisters, God is always with us and He goes in front of us to clear our path. We can do everything if we keep our eyes fixed on Him.

"Unto you it is given for Christ, not only to believe in Him but also to suffer for Him" (Philippians 1:29). We will suffer in this world, my brothers and sisters, there is no other choice, but let us use this suffering and unite it to the suffering of Jesus for His Glory and for the healing, conversion, and salvation of our brothers and sisters.

"For I reckon that the sufferings of this time are not worthy to be compared with the glory to come that shall be revealed in us" (Romans 8:18). This life is so short, we should not be afraid to carry our crosses. No matter how many times we fall, let us get up as Jesus did when He was carrying His cross. All the sufferings will pass, all of them my dear brothers and sisters, but the glory to come will be forever and ever.

St Alphonsus said, "We are aware of the fact that though the guilt of sin is remitted by a contrite confession, there still remains a temporal punishment to endure. If in the present life we neglect to make atonement, we shall have to suffer in the fire of purgatory." So, it is better for us to suffer and make up for our sins here on earth than in purgatory later.

Therefore, my brothers and sisters as St. Peter said to them: "Do penance, and be baptized every one of you in the name of Jesus Christ, for the remission of your sins: and you shall receive the gift of the Holy Ghost" (Acts of Apostles 2:28). We need to "Encourage ourselves to endure patiently the labors and affliction of this life, it is much less than the pains of purgatory. After all, God gives no more than what can be endured; and His Majesty gives patience first" (St. Teresa of Avila). Trust that Our Father will always give us all the graces necessary to carry all of our burdens.

Jesus tells us, "I came not to call the just, but sinners to penance" (Luke 5:32). We are all sinners and in need of penance to not only help save our souls but those of our brothers and sisters too. In doing our penance we will give joy to heaven as Jesus said, "I say to you, that even so there shall be joy in heaven upon one sinner that doth penance, more than upon ninety-nine just who need not penance" (Luke 15:7).

"By suffering we are able to give something to God." (St. Pio of Pietrelcina). "The Creator of the universe awaits the prayer, the immolation of one poor little soul to save a multitude of others, redeemed like her at the price of His Blood. Jesus has for us a love so incomprehensible that He does not wish to do anything without making us His co-operators. He wills that we should have a part with Him in the salvation of souls" (St. Therese of Lisiux). Let us take part in this great mission to suffer for souls as Jesus suffered for us.

Our Lady, the Virgin Mary told the Fatima children, "Pray, pray very much, and make sacrifices for sinners; for many souls go to hell, because there are none to sacrifice and to pray for them" (July 13, 1917). Souls go to hell because there is no one to pray and make sacrifices for them. So, let us use every opportunity to pray and make sacrifices for the souls of our dear brothers and sisters who are in so much danger of losing their souls to the fires of hell. Many people today more than ever need your prayers and sacrifices in order to obtain all the graces necessary for their healing, conversion, and salvation.

St. Veronica Giuliani related a vision she had about the infernal place, Hell, she said, "It seemed that many souls descend there, and they were so ugly and black that they struck terror in me. They all dropped down in a rush, one after the other and once they had entered those chasms there was nothing to be seen but fire and flames." These souls will be there for eternity. These are the souls of our brothers and sisters. It is as Our Lady of Fatima said, there was no one to pray and make sacrifices for them. But, right now you have the opportunity to do something about it. Do not pass it. The only thing that we take when we die is our souls. We must take care of them. Our mission should always be the salvation of souls through Jesus for the Glory of God. There is nothing more important that we could do in this world other than to work for the salvation of souls for whom Jesus gave up His Life on the Cross.

Our Lady of Lourdes is calling us to "Penance! Penance! Penance! Pray to God for sinners." Listen to the call Our Mother in Heaven who also prays for her dear children. Oh, my brothers and sisters pray very much and offer sacrifices for them.

Our Lord longs for souls as He Himself told St. Faustina, "I thirst. I thirst for the salvation of souls. Help me, my daughter, to save souls" (Diary of St. Faustina, 1032). One way we can help is by offering all of the suffering of our daily life in union with the suffering of Our Lord Jesus on the Cross for the salvation of souls. When we do this, our little offering becomes of great value because they are united to those of Our Lord. These little offerings will help our brothers and sisters obtain the graces necessary to save their souls and in doing so we also save our own soul as the Holy Scriptures say. "He should know that whoever brings back a sinner from the error of his way will save his soul from death and will cover a multitude of sins" (James 5:20).

"A great 'secret' of converting sinners is to make sacrifices for them, as well as to pray for them. The Holy Cure of Ars said that the conversion of sinners 'begins with prayers and ends with penance.' But whereas 'penance' and 'sacrifices' sounds frightening to some people and we may not like these words, yet they are the key to obtaining Heaven for poor sinners. If we are frightened of penance we can begin by making one little sacrifice per day — perhaps eating something we do not like, or drinking water instead of pop, or making ourselves wait a half hour or so to take a drink when we are thirsty. These are little forms of 'fasting.' Some sacrifices we are obliged to make, but we can offer them for sinners: examples of this are being patient with a trying person, or turning off an immodest TV program. These sacrifices will be presents for Our Lady, the precious coin she can use to buy back souls that are headed for Hell" (*From Devotion for the Dying* by Venerable Mother Mary Potter 233-234).

"Bring forth therefore fruit worthy of penance. And think not to say within yourselves, we have Abraham for our father. For I tell you that God is able of these stones to raise up children to Abraham. For now the axe is laid to the root of the trees. Every tree therefore that doth not yield good fruit, shall be cut down, and cast into the fire" (Matthew 3:8-10). Let us bear great fruit by helping our brothers and sisters save their souls for the Glory of God.

Here are some examples from Children who are now declared saints but we can surely follow the example of children.

Saint Jacinta of Fatima

Jacinta took this matter of making sacrifices for the conversion of sinners so much to heart, that she never let a single opportunity escape her. There were two families in Moita whose children used to go around begging from door to door. The Fatima children met them one day, as they were going along with their sheep. As soon as Jacinta saw them, she said, "Let's give our lunch to those children for the conversion of sinners." In addition, Jacinta would eat bitter acorns as a sacrifice. Lucia said to her, "Jacinta, don't eat that; it is too bitter!" "But it is because it is bitter that I am eating it, for the conversion of sinners."

On another occasion, on a very hot day, the sun was blazing and the Fatima Children were parched with thirst and there was not a single drop of water for them to drink. At first, they offered the sacrifice generously for the conversion of sinners, but after midday, they could not hold out any longer. They asked for a drink from a neighbor, but once they had received a pitcher they thought again of the conversion of sinners and gave the water to the sheep.

Venerable Anne de Guigne

"Nothing would stop her," writes Madame de Guigne, "when she meant to save a soul. She would sacrifice herself in countless little ways and never lost a chance of offering something to God for her poor sinner." Of course, Anne was too young to know much of the evil that exists in the world, but she knew it did exist and that nuns often came into contact with these wicked people, so she used to ask them to give her a soul to convert, a really big sinner, preferably. She would then listen gravely till she knew all about her sinner, then with a most businesslike air, she would say firmly: I will see about it — as though she had an understanding with Our Lord on the matter. Nothing discouraged the little apostle. If the sinner was obdurate, she prayed the harder and enlisted the whole family in a crusade of prayer. Resistance roused her zeal and she urged everyone to persevere till they had wretched the grace from God. "We must go on praying, Mother," she said when she heard that an obstinate old man, whose heart was as hard as the mountains amidst which he lived, still persisted in refusing the Sacraments in spite of all their prayers. Anne and her mother were just leaving church when they heard the news, but she wanted to go back and pray some more for her precious sinner. "I am determined that he shall go to confession," she insisted. "Let's go and pray some more." And she won the battle.

Here are some examples of sacrifices that can be made for the conversion of your brothers and sisters.

- Offer up your headaches and pains — emotional, physical, spiritual.
- Giving up your dessert or taking a smaller portion.
- Be patient instead of being mad or getting angry.
- Greeting those to whom you do not feel a particular liking to.
- Smiling when you feel like frowning.
- Talking when you feel like being silent.
- Listening when you feel like talking.
- Make a sacrifice of your regular work.
- If you are sick, offer up your sickness.
- Kneel when you feel like sitting when you are praying.
- Love when you don't feel like it and be extra loving to those around you.

Blessed Columba Marmion said, "Suffering is not the last word in the Christian life. After having shared in the Passion of the Savior, we shall also share in His glory." Upon the very eve of His Death, Jesus said to His Disciples: 'You are they who have continued with Me in My temptations. And I dispose to you, as My Father hath disposed to Me, a kingdom." The kingdom of Our Father in heaven waits for us and for our brothers and sisters, our true home. So, let us keep our eyes fixed on the goal, Heaven for this reason alone we were created.

Chapter 6

SAVING SOULS

"He must know that he who causeth a sinner to be converted from the error of his way will save his own soul from death and shall cover a multitude of sins" (James 5:19-20).

My brothers and sisters saving souls through Jesus for the Glory of God and for the love of our neighbor is the most important work we can do in this world. If you were able to invent a new medicine which would add ten years to every person living on this earth, while a great deed it pales in comparison to saving one soul which will live forever praising Our Lord in Heaven. That soul is so precious to God that He sent His only Son to die on the Cross. That soul is priceless to God and He is willing to pay any price to save a soul.

The following quotes are from "Win souls for Christ," by Our Lady of the Rosary Library:

St. John Chrysostom, (347-407), the illustrious Bishop of Constantinople, and Doctor of the Church, tells us: "Zeal for the salvation of souls is of so great a merit before God, that to give up all our goods to the poor, or to spend our whole life in the exercises of all sorts of austerities cannot equal the merit of it. There is no service more agreeable to God than this one. To employ one's life in this blessed labor is more pleasing to the Divine Majesty than to suffer martyrdom. Would you not feel happy if you could spend large sums of money in corporal works of mercy? But know that he who labors for the salvation of souls does far more; nay, the zeal of souls is of far greater merit before God ... than the working of miracles."

Pope St. Gregory the Great (590-604): "No sacrifice is more acceptable to God than zeal for souls."

St. Vincent de Paul (1576-1660): That St. Vincent was devoured by zeal for the house of God, his entire life testifies, because that life was employed in combating evil and extending the reign of good; and in this consists true zeal. Listen to some of his instructions to his community: "Let us give ourselves to God, gentlemen, to go to carry His holy Gospel over the entire earth and into whatever part He may lead us; there, let us maintain our part, and continue our duties until such time as His good pleasure will withdraw us. Let no difficulties move us, the glory of the eternal Father and the efficacy of the Word and of the passion of His Son are at stake. The salvation of men and our own are so great that they merit to be obtained at any price."

St. Rose of Lima, (1586-1617). We read that her confessor offered himself to go to the missions, but he feared because of the dangers it would entail. After consulting the saint, he heard these words: "Go Father, and do not fear. Leave all to labor for the conversion of the infidel, and know that the greatest service that man can offer to God is to convert souls, for this is a work proper of the Apostolate. What greater happiness could there be than to baptize, be it only a little Indian child who would enter Heaven through the gates of Baptism?"

St. John de Brebeuf (1593-1649), one of the eight North American Martyrs, was heard to say, after pouring the saving waters of Baptism on a dying Indian child, "For this one single occasion I would travel all the way from France; I would cross the great ocean to win one little soul for Our Lord!"

St. Margaret Mary (1647-1690): "My divine Savior has given to understand that those who work for the salvation of souls will have a gift of touching the most hardened hearts, and will labor with marvelous success, if they themselves are penetrated with a tender devotion to His Divine Heart."

Blessed Cardinal John Newman (1801-1890): "How can we answer to ourselves for the souls who have in our times lived and died in sin; the souls that have been lost and are now waiting for the judgment, seeing that for what we know, we were ordained to influence or reverse their present destiny and have not done it?"

St. Anthony Mary Claret (1808-1870): "Another thing that spurs me on to preach ceaselessly is the thought of the multitude of souls which fall into the depths of hell, who die in mortal sin, condemned forever and ever... if you were to see a blind man about to fall into a pit or over a precipice, would you not warn him? Behold, I do the same..." "How often I pray with **St. Catherine of Siena**: O my God, grant me a place by the gates of Hell, that I may stop those who enter there, saying: "Where are you going, unhappy one?

Back, go back! Make a good confession. Save your soul. Don't come here to be lost for all eternity!" **St. Anthony** resolved never to waste a moment of time, and during his 35 years as a priest, he wrote 144 books and preached some 25,000 sermons. On one trip, besides traveling, he preached 205 sermons in 48 days and 12 in one day.

The motivating force that dominated **St. John Bosco's** (1815-1888) life is found in a phrase that is typically his: "Give me souls, you take the rest." "There is nothing more holy in this world than to work for the good of souls, for whose salvation Jesus Christ poured out the last drops of His Blood." In his writings and conferences, he consistently pointed out that: "Man is successful in this world if he saves his soul and is very knowledgeable if he knows the science of salvation; but he is a total failure if he loses his soul and knows nothing if he is ignorant of those things that can assure him of eternal salvation." From his book *The Life of St. Dominic Savio*, St. John Bosco had this to say of St. Dominic Savio (the teenage saint who died in his 15th year): "The thought of saving souls for God was never out of his mind." St. Dominic Savio, (1842-1856), in a serious conversation with one of his companions, gave several reasons for his apostolic zeal in "saving souls": 1. My companion's soul has been redeemed by Jesus Christ. 2. We are all brothers and so we must love each other's souls. 3. God urges us to help each other. 4. If I manage to save one soul, I also ensure the salvation of my own.

St. Thérèse of Lisieux (1873-1897): "We have only short moments of this life to work for God's glory. The devil knows this and that is why he tries to make us waste time in useless things. O, let us not waste our time! Let us save souls! Souls are falling into hell innumerable as the flakes of snow on a winter day. Jesus weeps! Instead of consoling Him we are brooding over our own sorrows ... There is only one thing to do during the brief day, or rather, night of this life: Love Jesus with all the strength of your heart and save souls for Him, so that He may be loved!"

St. Pio (1887-1968): "Time spent in honor of God and for the salvation of souls is never badly spent."

St. Maximilian Kolbe (1894-1941): "We have no right to rest as long as a single soul is Satan's slave."

Our Lord to **St. Josefa Menendez** (1890-1923): "I am not attracted by your merits but by your love for souls." "When a soul is generous enough to give me all I ask, she gathers up treasures for herself and others and snatches great numbers of souls from perdition." " I so much want souls to understand this! It is not the action in itself that is of value; it is the intention with which it is done."

"Understand this well, Josefa: when a soul loves Me, she can make up for many who offend Me, and this relieves My Heart." "One faithful soul can repair and obtain mercy for many ungrateful ones." "A little act of generosity, of patience, of poverty ... may become treasure that will win a great number of souls to My Heart."

Our Lord to **Sr. Consolata Betrone** (1903-1946): "I prefer one act of love to all other prayers: 'Jesus, Mary, I love Thee! Save souls!' This comprises all: the souls in Purgatory, those in the Church Militant, the guilty and the innocent, the dying and the godless! One act of love can determine eternal happiness for a soul. Therefore, be careful never to omit one 'Jesus, Mary, I love Thee, Save Souls!' Do not lose time!

Every act of love means a soul! Our Lady told Sister Consolata, "Only in Heaven will you realize the value and the fruitfulness of saving souls. The act of love is especially meritorious as one of reparation."

Our Lord asked **St. Faustina**, to "Fight for the salvation of souls, exhorting them to trust in My mercy, as that is your task in this life and in the life to come" (Diary of St. Faustina 1452).

From *The Story of a Soul* by St Therese of the Child Jesus, page 42:

From that day the cry of my dying Savior — "I thirst!" — sounded incessantly in my heart, and kindled therein a burning zeal hitherto unknown to me. My one desire was to give my Beloved to drink; I felt myself consumed with thirst for souls, and I longed at any cost to snatch sinners from the everlasting flames of hell. In order still further to en-kindle my ardor, Our Divine Master soon proved to me how pleasing to him was my desire. Just then I heard much talk of a notorious criminal, Pranzini, who was sentenced to death for several shocking murders, and, as he was quite impenitent, everyone feared he would be eternally lost. How I longed to avert this irreparable calamity! In order to do so I employed all the spiritual means I could think of, and, knowing that my own efforts were unavailing, I offered for his pardon the infinite merits of Our Savior and the treasures of Holy Church. Need I say that in the depths of my heart I felt certain my request would be granted? But, that I might gain courage to persevere in the quest for souls, I said in all simplicity: "My God, I am quite sure that Thou wilt pardon this unhappy Pranzini. I should still think so if he did not confess his sins or give any sign of sorrow, because I have such confidence in Thy unbounded mercy; but this is my first sinner, and therefore I beg for just one sign of repentance to reassure me." My prayer was granted to the letter. My Father never allowed us to read the papers, but I did not think there was any disobedience in looking at the part about Pranzini. The day after his execution I hastily opened the paper, La Croix, and what did I see? Tears betrayed my emotion; I was obliged to run out of the room. Pranzini had mounted the scaffold without confessing or receiving absolution, and the executioners were already dragging him towards the fatal block, when all at once, apparently in answer to a sudden inspiration, he turned round, seized the crucifix which the Priest was offering to him, and kissed Our Lord's Sacred Wounds three times ... I had obtained the sign I asked for, and to me it was especially sweet. Was it not when I saw the Precious Blood flowing from the Wounds of Jesus that the thirst for souls first took possession of me? I wished to give them to drink of the Blood of the Immaculate Lamb that it might wash away their stains, and the lips of "my first born" had been pressed to these Divine Wounds. What a wonderful answer!

My dear brothers and sisters let us; start today to work for the salvation of souls. This is a mission of "LOVE." Let us, show Our Lord how much we love Him by helping our brothers and sisters save their souls through Jesus. In the next chapter, you will find a simple way to fight for the salvation of our brothers' and sisters' souls. There are many people going to hell because there is no one to pray for them. Know my brothers and sisters that Our Lord has promised through the revelation He made to St. Faustina, that He will always hear and answer the prayer for conversion of sinners. So, please raise your eyes to heaven and ask Our Heavenly Father for the grace of healing, conversion, and salvation of our brothers and sisters. Let us win souls for the glory of Our Lord Jesus Christ.

Hear the call of Our Lord Jesus Christ when He says, "You have not chosen Me: but I have chosen you; and have appointed you, that you should go, and should bring forth fruit; and your fruit should remain: that whatsoever you shall ask of the Father in My Name, He may give it you" (John 15:16). Let us bring forth fruit that shall remain forever, Souls!

Chapter 7

THE ADOPTION MOVEMENT

Our Lord told Saint Mechtilde, "If any one out of pure Love of God prays for another person as though he was praying for himself, his prayer shall enlighten the heavenly Jerusalem like the morning sun" (Devotion for the Dying, pages 22-23).

The Adoption Movement is a work of love and its mission is to help save souls for the Glory of God. There is nothing more important for a person to do other than to help save souls as well as his/her own through Jesus Christ. "Whoever brings back a sinner will save his soul from death and will cover a multitude of sins" (James 5:20). Our Lord Jesus told Saint Faustina, "I thirst. I thirst for the salvation of souls. Help me, my daughter, to save souls. Join your sufferings to My Passion and offer them to the heavenly Father for sinners" (Diary of St. Faustina 1032). Please let us help Our Dear Lord Jesus Christ quench His thirst by helping Him bring his dear children home, like the prodigal son.

Our Lord Jesus told St. Faustina, "The prayer most pleasing to Me is the prayer of conversion of sinners. Know my daughter that this prayer is always heard and answered" (Diary of St. Faustina 1397). We should be confident that Our Lord will answer our prayers when we pray for the healing, conversion, and salvation of our brothers and sisters. "This is good and pleasing to God our Savior, who wills everyone to be saved and to come to knowledge of the truth" (1 Timothy 2:3-4). "We have this confidence in Him, that if we ask anything according to His will, He hears us. And if we know that He hears us in regard to whatever we ask, we know that what we have asked Him for is ours" (1 John 5:14-15). It is that simple my brothers and sisters, just ask and we shall receive it. Trust in the Words of Our Lord.

The Adoption Movement involves the spiritual adoption of anyone who touches your heart as your brother or sister. All you have to do is to pray the adoption prayer and solemnly promise Our Lord Jesus Christ to pray and make sacrifices for your new spiritually adopted brother(s) or sister(s) for the rest of your life. It is recommendable that you write their name down or a description of that person if you do not know their name, that way you will never forget them. You can add more names as you start to spiritually adopt more people to your spiritually adopted list. Our Lady, the Virgin Mary told the Fatima children, "Pray, Pray very much, and make sacrifices for sinners; for many souls go to hell, because there are none to sacrifice and to pray for them" (July 13, 1917). My dear brothers and sisters, please join me today in this mission of "Love." Let us, start today to spiritually adopt our dear family members, our friends, our priests, our enemies, strangers, our towns, our cities, our parish, our country, etc. The whole world needs you more than ever before. We are all created in the image of Our Lord Jesus Christ, so let us look beyond color, race, age, religion, etc. "For those who are led by the Spirit of God are children of God. For you did not receive the spirit of slavery to fall back into fear, but received the Spirit of adoption, through which we cry, 'Abba, Father!' The Spirit itself bears witness with our spirit that we are the children of God" (Romans 8:14-16). "And I will receive you; and I will be a Father to you; and you shall be my sons and daughters, saith the Lord Almighty" (2 Corinthians 6:18). Therefore, we are all the sons and daughters of God and consequently brothers and sisters.

The greatest spiritual adoption that ever occurred is when the Virgin Mary stood under the Cross of Calvary as her Son was dying for our salvation. Speaking of John, Jesus told His Mother, "This is your son." To John, He said of Mary, "This is your Mother." The apostle John represented all of us. On that Good Friday, therefore, Christ made His Mother the supernatural Mother of the human race and made us her spiritual children. Let us follow the example of Our Dear Mother Mary who has adopted us all at the foot of the Cross. Please join in this great battle to help save souls by spiritually adopting our brothers and sisters for the Glory of God. Choose someone who touches your heart and spiritually adopt them now: (***prayer on next page***).

ADOPTION PRAYER

*In the Name of the Father, the Son, and the Holy Spirit. Amen.
Come Holy Ghost, Creator Blest, And in our hearts take up Thy rest;
Come with Thy grace and heav'nly aid To fill the hearts which Thou
hast made, To fill the hearts which Thou hast made.*

*O Comfort Blest to Thee we cry, Thou heav'nly Gift of God most high;
Thou fount of life and fire of love, And sweet anointing from above,
And sweet anointing from above.*

*Saint Michael the Archangel, defend us in battle. Be our defense
against the wickedness and snares of the devil. May God rebuke him,
we humbly pray; and do Thou, O Prince of the Heavenly Host - by the
Power of God thrust into hell, satan and all the evil spirits, who prowl
about the world seeking the ruin of souls. Amen.*

*My sweet Jesus, my God and my Savior, I solemnly adopt (Name of
Adoptee(s)) as my spiritual brother/sister and promise to pray and
make sacrifices for the rest of my life and into eternity for him/her
and all my adopted brothers and sisters.*

*O Jesus, who has said, "Ask and you shall receive, seek and you shall
find, knock and it will be opened to you," Behold I ask, I seek, and I
knock for that faith that obtains all and for the healing, conversion,
and salvation of all my adopted brothers and sisters.*

*In the name of Jesus, I cast out all evil spirits that are hindering the
healing, conversion, and salvation of my adoptee(s) to go directly to
the foot of the cross bound in Jesus' hands without doing any harm
to me or my family, to be sent by Him to the deepest recesses of hell.
Never to come back, never to come back,
never to come back. (Three times)*

The Adoption Movement

Oh! Most Holy Trinity, Father, Son, and Holy Spirit, I adore Thee profoundly. I offer Thee the most precious Body, Blood, Soul and Divinity of Jesus Christ, present in all the tabernacles of the world, in reparation for the outrages, sacrileges and indifferences by which He is offended. By the infinite merits of the Sacred Heart of Jesus and the Immaculate Heart of Mary, I beg the conversion of poor sinners, especially my adopted brothers and sisters. Amen.

Most merciful Jesus, you revealed to Saint Faustina that whoever calls upon your mercy on behalf of a poor sinner and said this prayer with a contrite heart and faith will be given the grace of his/her conversion. Behold I now pray with confidence in your mercy for my adoptee(s) "O Blood and Water which gushed forth from the Heart of Jesus as a fountain of mercy for us I trust in You."

Dear St. Joseph I ask you to please adopt me, my family, and my adoptee(s) as your sons and daughters forever.
Sweet Virgin Mary as you adopted the Beloved Disciple at the foot of the cross, I ask you to adopt me, my family, and my adoptee(s) as your beloved sons and daughters forever.

Divino Nino, raise your Holy Arms for us and bless us.
Jesus, Mary, and Joseph, I love you, save souls.
Jesus, my God and my All, I trust in you and I will sing your praises forever and ever. Amen.

Chip, Rebecca, Toby, Maureen, Sissi, Patty, Louise, Joe, John, Jane, Joan, David, Richard, Elaine & Dennis, Connie, Laura, Dolly, Joyce, Lois, Pat, Roger, Lor. D., Lor. V., Betty, K., (57) and all their families for 5 generations + FB friends

Chapter 8

DIFFERENT TYPES OF SPIRITUAL ADOPTIONS

"When Jesus saw his mother, and the disciple whom he loved standing near, he said to his mother, 'Woman, behold, your son!' Then he said to the disciple, Behold, your mother!" (John 19:26-27).

My dear brothers and sisters, adoption speaks of love, mercy, and grace. In this world, adoption it is a legal action whereby a person is brought into a family in which he has no blood relations. In this case, it is not by a legal action but it is by "love" alone that brings us to the Family of God.

There are several ways one can start to spiritual adopt our brothers and sisters.

1. Single adoption: This is when we spiritually adopt one person at a time. For instance, you can adopt anyone as your brother, sister, mother, father, son, or daughter, grandmother, grandfather, etc. In addition, single adoption includes family members, friends, acquaintances, priests, neighbors, strangers, enemies especially because The Holy Ghost revealed to us in the Gospel of Matthew 5:44, "But I say to you, Love your enemies: do good to them that hate you: and pray for them that persecute and calumniate you." Our Lord Jesus Christ, when hanging on the Cross and suffering the most excruciating pains, prayed for the greatest sinners and His enemies: "Father, forgive them, for they know not what they do" (Luke 23:34). What better example than Our Lord Himself praying for His enemies. Our Lord wants us to pray for each other in order to help each other to save our souls. St. Therese of the Child Jesus inspired by the Holy Spirit one day decided to pray for a notorious criminal named Pranzini who was sentenced to death. She adopted Pranzini as "Her first born." In the book of James, Chapter 5, verse 16 says: "Confess therefore your sins one to another: and pray one for another, that you may be saved. For the continual prayer of a just man availeth much." If you want to do the Will of Our Father in heaven, my dear brothers and sisters we must pray for each other that we might be saved and one day became the family that Our Lord Jesus Christ wants us to be. We are our brothers keeper, let us not be like Cain who said to the Lord, "Cain: Where is thy brother Abel? And he answered, I know not: am I my brother's keeper?" "For you are all the children of God by faith, in Christ Jesus" (Galatians 3:26). We are all brothers and sisters.

2. Family or group adoption: This is when we adopt a whole family at the same time or a group of people. You can adopt them as your brothers, sisters, sons, daughters, etc. Family or group adoption can include: Your whole parish, all your co-workers, your child's class, a school, a city, any state, any country, people suffering from cancer, the archdiocese of your church, etc. It can be any group that might touch your heart. Methuen, USA, Israel,
Boston Archb., Jews

The adoption movement is not only for people who are not in the faith. It is for everyone because even if we already

Sr Ctr

60

are in the faith we need prayers to persevere and grow in God's grace. As Fr. d'Elbee says in his book, I Believe in Love, page 178, "Do not ask only for the return of sinners, but that good people will become very good, and that the very good will become saints." For instance, when we adopt a priest, we pray for his ministry and for him to be able to carry out his mission which is to save souls through Jesus. St. Therese of the Child Jesus adopted two missionary priests as her brothers. She offered prayers and sacrifices in order for them to carry out their mission in life and grow in God's love. *I adopt JMT + Viola (Spiritual Parents*

Different adoption examples

- Your doctor *— DRS - Dolly, Klein, Pisick*
- Your cousin
- Your neighbor *5 - all*
- Your child's teacher
- Your enemies *~ M*
- A criminal you heard about on the news
- A terrorist *~ all ISIS*
- Your mother's friend
- Your archbishop *— Sean*
- The victims of natural disasters
- The soldiers in both sides of the war *✓*
- All the members of Confirmation class */ BSC/D*
- Your country
- Your parish *~ St M*
- Anyone that touches your heart, etc. *Lor, D, Rosa,*

Marit zu, Lynn, Zach, Annmarie, Carmen fam, MIKE Scannell Deanna + fam., all BSC/D, all Parishoners, All St Bas. (Fr. Martin + all, inc, DeColores Eddie, Ray, Fred ROSA, Mareinie

The more you pray and sacrifice for others the closer to Jesus you become. For example: You start to trust more in the mercy of God. People become precious to you because you will understand the value of a single soul to God. The value of a soul to God is worth the supreme Sacrifice on Calvary. The people you adopt become your family, they will truly become your brothers and sisters as Our Lord want us to be. In every person you see you can see Jesus. You can see beyond the face and body, you see their souls. Sacrifice for those you love becomes sweet. To pray always and offer sacrifices in union with the suffering of Jesus to our Father in Heaven for the healing, conversation, and salvation of our brothers and sisters for the glory of Our Lord Jesus Christ should always be on our minds. As St. Alphonsus said that souls who "really love God will never neglect to pray for sinners." So let us show our love for Our Lord and Savior by helping our brothers and sisters save their souls by offering our prayers and sacrifices through the only way, Jesus.

The Chateau, Toby's Store, Court where Kelly works, Mystic where Rosa works, Judy & where she works in England

Chapter 9

HOW THE ADOPTION MOVEMENT BEGAN

A mission of "Love"

After reading *The Life of Venerable Anne De Guigne*, she inspired me to love sinners. Anne would pray for their conversion with all her heart. She prayed until they were converted. Ever since I was a small girl I had a great desire to work for God. I wanted to use my life for His Glory. My soul was thirsty. Nothing satisfied my longing for my God. I have the need to be useful for God's Glory. I wished I could have been a nun or missionary or a great heroine like Joan of Arc, but God called me to the married life instead. My desire to work for the Lord was still burning in my heart more and more. Now, I desired to become a servant since I could not be anything I wished I could have been. I felt a call to pray for the conversion of sinners. While in church at a Sunday Mass, I looked up to see the painting of Our Lady and to my surprise, I heard Our Lady say in my heart that she wanted me to pray for sinners, but to pray for them as if they were part of my own family, my own brothers and sisters. There was a man at my parish that would drive his wife to daily Mass everyday and wait in his car for her. On Sundays he would go to Mass but he would not receive Jesus Christ in the Eucharist. It would break my heart every time I saw him because he was so close and yet so far. This man reminded me of my earthly father whom I loved so much. I saw him every Sunday since we went to the same Mass. I felt called to adopt him as my first spiritually adopted father. I asked Our Lady if she would take me as her servant. I wanted to serve Jesus with all my heart through her, and I asked her for a sign that she would accept my poor insignificant offering. The sign was that I would see this poor man, my first spiritually adopted father receive Jesus Christ in the Holy Eucharist. Day after day I prayed for my adopted father especially during the Consecration at Mass. I prayed with all my heart to the point that my heart would hurt. Since I did not know his name I wrote a description on a piece of paper which I put under a statue of Our Lady and his name for me was 'My adopted father." The more I prayed for him the greater the desire help him to save his soul. I offered my communions for his conversion, I added him to my daily prayers, I asked my family to pray for him, etc. My love for my adopted father grew more and more each day. After praying for him for a while I started to really see him like my real earthly father. After six months, Our Lady, The Virgin Mary gave me the most beautiful surprise, it was Christmas Day 2004, She had finally accepted my poor offering. I saw her statue smile at me; my adopted father went up and received Our Lord's Body and Blood. I was unable to hold my tears. The happiness in my heart was inexplicable. I felt such a great joy. I have never been so happy in my entire life. I knew at that moment I had become Our Lady's servant. I knew at that moment that I had found my vocation, to work for the salvation of my brothers and sisters. I pledged to her that I would do everything I can to help save souls through her Son, Jesus Christ. In my heart there is an incredible desire to pray for sinners. In my heart, there is a warrior for souls. This is the work that my heart has been thirsting for all my life until now. I want to fight for the salvation of all of my brothers and sisters. After my adopted fathers conversion I started to adopt more sinners as well as people in the faith. I pray for them and make sacrifices everyday and I know with the intercession of Our Lady my adopted family will be healed, converted, and saved and one day we will all rejoice in God's Kingdom forever. I also have adopted you who are reading this book as my dear brother or sister.

Fruits of the Adoption

1. Conversion of your brothers and sisters. The very first person I adopted, after six months of prayer, The Lord Jesus answered my prayer and I witnessed him receiving Jesus Christ in the Eucharist on Christmas day.

2. Your enemies become your friends. For example: My husband almost got into a fight with a man because of different views on Chiropractic and in-vitro fertilization. My husband adopted the older man as his father in his heart and a year later they ran into each other and the other man had forgotten the disagreement and was like a long lost family friend to our family.

Casey Mitchell, Mother of Servants of JM I now adopt you back, my sister, Esmeralda Kiezek + your whole family inc. all those you adopted

3. Love of God and neighbor. By praying for our brothers and sisters, we fulfill the two greatest commandments given to us by God, which are: "Thou shalt love the Lord thy God with thy whole heart, and with thy whole soul, and with thy whole mind. This is the greatest and the first commandment. And the second is like to this: Thou shalt love thy neighbor as thyself. On these two commandments dependeth the whole law and the prophets" (Matthew 22:37-40). We can show God, we love Him by obeying the second commandment which is to love our neighbor as ourselves. We can show God we love our neighbors by praying and making sacrifices in order to help them save their souls. We preach charity toward the poor and unfortunate people. That is beautiful, and it must be done; and yet, what is material charity when compared to a soul? I refer to the conquering of even one soul, for there is nothing greater than that - to conquer souls redeemed by Our Lord, for whom He shed His Precious Blood. That is true gratitude, true charity.

4. Victory over all enemies. We need to start today to pray and offer sacrifices for our brothers and sisters. Many of us need your prayers today. Jesus said, "But seek first the kingdom of [God] and his righteousness, and all these things will be given you besides" (Matthew 6:33). If you want abortion to end, to have peace in this world, to stop hunger, to stop crimes, we need to start praying and sacrificing for our brothers' and sisters' souls so that our Dear Lord may grant them the grace of conversion, and then I truly believe that all these bad things will change because our brothers' and sisters' hearts would be changed. God thirsts for souls, so your prayers and sacrifices will quench His thirst. It won't be easy, but if we all join forces and start to spiritually adopt and offer prayers and sacrifices for our brothers and sisters, we will win this battle against evil.

The more people who join the Adoption Movement, the more conversions will be obtained by the Grace of God. Please pray for the spread of the Adoption Movement, so one day, every person in the whole world will truly become one family united in the Love of God, Our Father.

-

Chapter 10

POWERFUL PRAYERS TO SAVE SOULS

Jesus said to St. Faustina, "Help Me, My daughter, to save souls"
(Diary of St, Faustina 1032).

The Holy Mass

"The Holy Mass is the greatest wonder in the world. There is nothing on Earth equal to it, and is nothing in Heaven greater than it. The Mass is the same as the sacrifice of Calvary. It has the same infinite value of Calvary and brings down in all men the same priceless graces. St Augustine says that 'In the Mass the Blood of Christ flows anew for sinners.' The efficacy of the Mass is so wonderful, God's mercy and generosity are then so unlimited, that there is no moment so propitious to ask for favors as when Jesus is born on the altar. What we then ask we shall almost certainly receive. My brothers and sisters, we can do nothing better for the conversion of sinners than offer for them the Holy Sacrifice of the Mass" (*The Wonders of the Mass* by Fr. Paul O'Sullivan, O.P). Let us, offer Mass for the healing, conversion, and salvation of our adopted brothers and sisters as well as our own. This is the greatest thing we can ever do for the salvation of all of us.

The Holy Rosary

Besides the Indulgences attached to the Rosary, Our Lady revealed to St. Dominic and Blessed Alan de la Roche additional promises for those who devoutly pray the Rosary. Our Lady said, "You shall obtain all you ask of me by recitation of the Rosary." In addition, Sister Lucia (Fatima Seer) said regarding the Rosary, "There is no problem no matter how difficult it may be that cannot be solved by the recitation of the Holy Rosary." So, let us ask for the healing, conversion, and salvation of our dear adopted brothers and sisters.

The Holy Rosary

1. Make the Sign of the Cross and pray the "Apostle's Creed"
I believe in God, the Father Almighty, Creator of Heaven and earth; and in Jesus Christ, His only Son Our Lord, Who was conceived by the Holy Spirit, born of the Virgin Mary, suffered under Pontius Pilate, was crucified, died, and was buried. He descended into Hell; the third day He rose again from the dead; He ascended into Heaven, and sitteth at the right hand of God, the Father almighty; from thence He shall come to judge the living and the dead. I believe in the Holy Spirit, the holy Catholic Church, the communion of saints, the forgiveness of sins, the resurrection of the body and life everlasting. Amen.

2. Pray the "Our Father"

Our Father, Who art in heaven, Hallowed be Thy Name. Thy Kingdom come. Thy Will be done, on earth as it is in Heaven. Give us this day our daily bread. And forgive us our trespasses, as we forgive those who trespass against us. And lead us not into temptation, but deliver us from evil. Amen.

3. Pray three "Hail Marys"

Hail Mary, full of grace, the Lord is with thee; Blessed art thou among women, and blessed is the fruit of thy womb, Jesus. Holy Mary, Mother of God, pray for us sinners, now and at the hour of death. Amen.

4. Pray the "Glory Be To The Father"

GLORY BE to the Father, and to the Son, and to the Holy Spirit. As it was in the beginning, is now, and ever shall be, world without end. Amen.

5. Announce the First Mystery:

On Monday and Saturday, meditate on the "Joyful Mysteries"
First Decade: The Annunciation of Gabriel to Mary
(Luke 1:26-38)
Second Decade: The Visitation of Mary to Elizabeth
(Luke 1:39-56)
Third Decade: The Birth of Our Lord (Luke 2:1-21)
Fourth Decade: The Presentation of Our Lord (Luke 2:22-38)
Fifth Decade: The Finding of Our Lord in the Temple
(Luke 2:41-52)

On Thursday, meditate on the "Luminous Mysteries"
First Decade: The Baptism of Our Lord in the River Jordan
   (Matthew 3:13-16)
Second Decade: The Wedding at Cana, when Christ manifested
   Himself (John 2:1-11)
Third Decade: The Proclamation of the Kingdom of God
   (Mark 1:14-15)
Fourth Decade: The Transfiguration of Our Lord
   (Matthew 17:1-8)
Fifth Decade: The Last Supper, when Our Lord gave us the Holy
   Eucharist (Matthew 26)

On Tuesday and Friday, meditate on the "Sorrowful Mysteries"
First Decade: The Agony of Our Lord in the Garden
   (Matthew 26:36-56)
Second Decade: Our Lord is Scourged at the Pillar
   (Matthew 27:26)
Third Decade: Our Lord is Crowned with Thorns
   (Matthew 27:27-31)
Fourth Decade: Our Lord Carries the Cross to Calvary
   (Matthew 27:32)
Fifth Decade: The Crucifixion of Our Lord
   (Matthew 27:33-56)

On Wednesday and Sunday, meditate on the "Glorious Mysteries"
First Decade: The Glorious Resurrection of Our Lord
   (John 20:1-29)
Second Decade: The Ascension of Our Lord (Luke 24:36-53)
Third Decade: The Descent of the Holy Spirit at Pentecost
   (Acts 2:1-41)
Fourth Decade: The Assumption of Mary into Heaven
Fifth Decade: The Coronation of Mary as Queen of Heaven and
   Earth

6. Pray the "Our Father"

7. Pray ten "Hail Marys" while meditating on the Mystery.

8. Pray the "Glory Be To The Father"
> After each decade say the following prayer requested by the Blessed Virgin Mary at Fatima:

> *"O my Jesus, forgive us our sins, save us from the fires of hell, lead all souls to Heaven, especially those who have most need of your mercy."*

Announce the Second Mystery; then say the "Our Father" Repeat 6 , 7, 8, and 9 and continue with Third, Fourth and Fifth Mysteries in the same manner.

After the Rosary:

HAIL, HOLY QUEEN, Mother of Mercy, our life, our sweetness and our hope! To thee do we cry, poor banished children of Eve; to thee do we send up our sighs, mourning and weeping in this valley of tears. Turn then, most gracious advocate, thine eyes of mercy toward us, and after this our exile, show unto us the blessed fruit of thy womb, Jesus. O clement, O loving, O sweet Virgin Mary!

V. Pray for us, O Holy Mother of God.

R. That we may be made worthy of the promises of Christ. Let us pray. O GOD, whose only begotten Son, by His life, death, and resurrection, has purchased for us the rewards of eternal life, grant, we beseech Thee, that meditating upon these mysteries of the Most Holy Rosary of the Blessed Virgin Mary, we may imitate what they contain and obtain what they promise, through the same Christ Our Lord. Amen.

The Divine Mercy of God

This powerful devotion was given to St. Faustina in the early 1900's. Our Lord promised that through the Chaplet of Divine Mercy, we can obtain anything if it is compatible with God's Will. My brothers and sisters we know that God wills everyone to be saved. So, let us have confidence that through the Chaplet of Divine Mercy we will obtain the healing, conversion, and salvation of our adopted brothers and sisters.

"Say unceasingly this chaplet that I have taught you. Anyone who says it will receive great Mercy at the hour of death. Priests will recommend it to sinners as the last hope. Even the most hardened sinner, if he recites this Chaplet even once, will receive grace from My Infinite Mercy. I want the whole world to know My Infinite Mercy. I want to give unimaginable graces to those who trust in My Mercy... "(Diary of St. Faustina, 687).

The Chaplet of The Divine Mercy

1. Begin with the Sign of the Cross, Pray one Our Father, one Hail Mary and The Apostles Creed. Using a Rosary.

2. Then on the Our Father Beads say the following:

Eternal Father, I offer You the Body and Blood, Soul and Divinity of Your Dearly beloved Son, Our Lord Jesus Christ, in atonement for our sins and those of the whole world.

3. On the 10 Hail Mary Beads say the following:

For the sake of His sorrowful Passion, have mercy on us and on the whole world.

(Repeat step 2 and 3 for all five decades).

4. Conclude with (three times):

> *Holy God, Holy Mighty One, Holy Immortal One, have mercy on us and on the whole world.*

The Holy Face of Jesus

This devotion was given to Sister Mary of St. Peter in the 1800's by Jesus Christ Himself. Some of the promises for those who honor His Holy Face are:

1. By offering My Face to My Eternal Father, nothing will be refused, and the conversion of many sinners will be obtained.

2. By My Holy Face, they will work wonders, appease the anger of God and draw down mercy on sinners.

3. As in a kingdom they can procure all that is desired with a coin stamped with the King's effigy, so in the Kingdom of Heaven they will obtain all they desire with the precious coin of My Holy Face.

We can honor the Holy Face of Jesus to obtain the healing, conversion, and salvation of all our dear adopted brothers and sisters. Because Jesus has promised that nothing will be refused and the conversion of many sinners will be obtained.

Offering To The Holy Face

Eternal Father, I offer Thee the Adorable Face of Thy Beloved Son, for the honor and glory of Thy Name, for the conversion of sinners and for the salvation of the dying. I pray especially for all my dear adopted brothers and sisters.

Holy Face Prayer for Sinners
by St. Therese of Lisieux

Eternal Father, since thou has given me for my inheritance the Adorable Face of Thy Divine Son, I offer that Face to Thee. I beg Thee in exchange for this Coin of infinite value to forget the ingratitude of souls dedicated to Thee and to pardon all poor sinners especially all my dear adopted brothers and sisters.

The Golden Arrow

This prayer was dictated by Our Lord to Sister Mary of St. Peter. After receiving this prayer, Sister Mary of St. Peter was given a vision in which she saw the Sacred Heart of Jesus delightfully wounded by this "Golden Arrow," as torrents of graces streamed from It for the conversion of sinners.

May the most holy, most sacred, most adorable, most incomprehensible and unutterable Name of God be always praised, blessed, loved, adored and glorified, in Heaven, on earth, and under the earth, by all the creatures of God, and by the Sacred Heart of Our Lord Jesus Christ in the Most Holy Sacrament of the Altar. Amen.

The Precious Blood of Jesus

Our Lord told Sister Mary of St. Peter, "Ask My Father for as many souls as I shed drops of Blood during My Passion." There were 28,430 drops of blood lost by Our Lord. So, let us offer the blood of Our Lord Jesus Christ for the healing, conversion, and the salvation of our dear adopted brothers and sisters.

Precious Blood Offering

Eternal Father, I offer Thee the most Precious Blood of Jesus Christ, in satisfaction for my sins, in supplication for the holy souls in Purgatory and for the need of the Holy Church and especially for my dear adopted brothers and sisters.

Marian offering of the Precious Blood of Jesus Immaculate Heart of Mary, do thou offer to the Eternal Father the Precious Blood of Our Lord Jesus Christ, for the conversion of sinners, especially our dear adopted brothers and sisters.

Prayer of St. Gertrude the Great

Our Lord dictated the following prayer to St. Gertrude the Great to release 1,000 Souls from Purgatory each time it is said. The souls in Purgatory whom we have released through our prayers are sure to pray for our dear adopted brothers and sisters.

"Eternal Father, I offer Thee the Most Precious Blood of Thy Divine Son, Jesus, in union with the masses said throughout the world today, for all the holy souls in Purgatory, for sinners everywhere, for sinners in the universal church, those in my own home and within my family. Amen."

Blessed souls of Purgatory who are so dear to God, and who are secure of never losing Him, please pray for our dear adopted brothers and sisters. Amen.

The Holy Wounds of Jesus

This devotion was given to by Our Lord to sister Mary Martha of Chambon during the 1800's. It carries great promises to those who have a devotion to the Holy Wounds of Jesus. Some of these promises are:

1. At each word that you pronounce of the Chaplet of the Holy Wounds, I allow a drop of My Blood to fall upon the soul of a sinner.

2. I will grant all that is asked of Me through the invocation of My Holy Wounds. You will obtain everything, because it is through the merit of My Blood, which is of infinite price. With My Wounds and My Divine Heart, everything can be obtained.

3. A sinner who will say the following prayer will obtain conversion: "Eternal Father, I offer Thee the Wounds of our Lord Jesus Christ to heal those of our souls."

4. This chaplet is a counterpoise to My justice; it restrains My vengeance.

So, let us ask for the healing, conversion, and salvation of our dear brothers and sisters through the invocation of His Holy Wounds.

The Chaplet of The Holy Wounds

To be prayed using the Rosary beads
On the crucifix and first three beads:

O JESUS, Divine Redeemer, be merciful to us and to the whole world. Amen.

STRONG God, holy God, immortal God, have mercy on us and on the whole world. Amen.

GRACE and mercy, O my Jesus, during present dangers; cover us with Thy Precious Blood. Amen.

ETERNAL Father, grant us mercy through the Blood of Jesus Christ, Thine only Son; grant us mercy, we beseech Thee. Amen, Amen, Amen.

The following prayers, composed by Our Lord, are to be said using the Rosary beads.

On the Our Father beads:

Eternal Father, I offer Thee the Wounds of our Lord Jesus Christ. To heal the wounds of our souls.

On the Hail Mary beads:

My Jesus, pardon and mercy. Through the merits of Thy Holy Wounds.

The Angel's Prayer

Taught by an Angel to the children of Fatima.

Most Holy Trinity, Father, Son, and Holy Spirit, I adore Thee profoundly. I offer Thee the Most Precious Body, Blood, Soul and Divinity of Jesus Christ, present in all the tabernacles of the world, in reparation for the outrages, sacrileges and indifference by which He is offended. And through the infinite merits of His Most Sacred Heart, and the Immaculate Heart of Mary, I beg of Thee the conversion of poor sinners, especially my dear adopted brothers and sisters.

A Little Act of Entrusting a Soul to the Immaculate Heart of Mary

Immaculate Heart of Mary, I entrust to thee the salvation of (especially all my dear adopted brothers and sisters), having great confidence that thou wilt save them.

Divino Nino

One of the promises of The Child Jesus was revealed to Ven. Sister Margaret of the Blessed Sacrament, "Ask all that you desire through the merits of My Holy Infancy, Nothing will be refused."

Prayer to Divino Nino

Nihil Obstat: October 28, 2011 by Reverend Monsignor William Benwell Vicar General Diocese of Metuchen

My sweet little Child Jesus, You are my God and my Savior who has said,"Ask and you shall receive, seek and you shall find, knock and it will be opened to you." Behold I ask, I seek, and I knock for that faith that obtains all, as well as my special request for the healing, conversion, and salvation of my adopted brothers and sisters.

Divino Nino I want to hold you in my arms and love you forever. I promise in thanksgiving for answering my prayer to spread devotion to You in word and deed. My dear Child Jesus, I will sing your praises forever, and ever. Amen.

The Way of the Cross

This devotion was given to Brother Estanislas (1903-1927). Our Lord revealed great promises to those who have a devotion to the Way of the Cross. One of those promises is: "I will grant everything that is asked of Me with faith, when making The Way of the Cross." So, let us ask through the Way of the Cross for the healing, conversion, and salvation of all of dear adopted brothers and sisters.

The Way of the Cross
Opening Prayer

Lord Jesus Christ, take me along that holy way you once took to your death, Take my mind, my memory, above all my reluctant heart, and let me see what once you did for love of me and all the world.

To pray the Way of the Cross requires only that you meditate before each station. Before each station you may say:

We adore you, O Christ, and we bless you, because by your holy cross, you have redeemed the world.

After each station you may say: One Our Father, one Hail Mary, and one Glory Be ...

The 14 stations are:

1. Jesus is Condemned to Die
2. Jesus is Made to Bear His Cross
3. Jesus Falls the First Time
4. Jesus Meets His Mother
5. Simon Helps Jesus Carry His Cross
6. Veronica Wipes Jesus' Face
7. Jesus Falls the Second Time
8. Jesus Meets the Women of Jerusalem
9. Jesus Falls the Third Time
10. Jesus is Stripped
11. Jesus is Nailed to the Cross
12. Jesus Dies on the Cross
13. Jesus is taken down from the Cross
14. Jesus is buried in the Tomb

My dear brothers and sisters, "Pray, Pray very much, and make sacrifices for sinners" (Our Lady of Fatima).

Sources for Texts

1. Anne, The Life of Ven Anne de Guigne by Benecdictine Nun of Stanbrook Abbey, Tan Books and Publishers, Inc. Rockford, Illinois 61105, 1997.

2. Catechism of the Catholic Church, Second Edition by Libreria Editice Vaticana

3. Devotion to the Dying, Mary's Call to Her Loving Children by Ven. Mother Mary Potter. Tan Books and Publishers, Inc. Rockford, Illinois 61105, 1991. (Public Domain)

4. Divine Mercy in My Soul, The Diary of the Servant of God Sister M. Faustina Kowalska by Marian Press, Stockbridge, Massachusetts 01263, 1987.

5. Douay Rheims Catholic Bible. http://www.drbo.org/

6. I Believe in Love by Father Jean C. J. d'Elbee. Sophia Institute Press, Manchester, New Hampshire, 1974.

7. I Wait For You, Jesus Laments Over Man's Indifference by Tan Books and Publishers, Inc. Rockford, Illinois 61105, 1985.

8. Prayer The Key to Salvation by Father Michael Mueller, C.SS.R. Tan Books and Publishers, Inc. Rockford, Illinois 61105, 1985.

9. The Story of a Soul (L'Histoire d'une Âme): The Autobiography of St. Thérèse of Lisieux eBook. http://www.bookrags.com/ebooks/16772/42.html

10. The New American Bible by World Catholic Press.

11. The Wonders of the Mass by Father Paul O'Sullivan, O.P. (E.D.M). Tan Books and Publishers, Inc. Rockford, Illinois 61105, 1993.

12. Win Souls For Christ by Our Lady of the Rosary Library, 11721 Hidden Creek Road, Prospect, KY 40059. http://www.olrl.org/misc/

And Jesus told Sister Josefa Menendez to: "Realize the value of souls; consecrate yourself to giving this glory to the Blessed Trinity, by gaining many souls in which the Triune God may find a dwelling. Every soul can be instrumental in this sublime work. Nothing great is required, the smallest acts suffice: a step taken, a straw picked up, a glance restrained, a service rendered, a cordial smile ... all these offered to Love are in reality of great profit to souls and draw down floods of grace on them. No need to remind you of the fruits of prayer, of sacrifice, or any act offered to expiate the sins of mankind ... to obtain for them the grace of purification, that they too may become fitting sanctuaries for the indwelling of the Blessed Trinity" (I Wait For You, by Tan Books pp 26).

Dear Jesus & Mary
    Create in my heart &
soul an indwelling of your
    Blessed Trinity as Your
Blessed Sanctuary.

At the end of your life, may the Kings of Kings say to you:
"Come, ye blessed of my Father, possess you the kingdom prepared
for you from the foundation of the world. Amen I say to you, as
long as you did it to one of these my least brethren, you did it to me"
(Matthew 25:34 & 40).

ABOUT THE AUTHOR

Esmeralda Kiczek was born in El Salvador, Central America in the 1970's. In 1989, she came to the United States with her siblings to join her father who had come to the United States, ten years prior. Her father left El Salvador when Esmeralda was only five years old and he traveled to the USA in search for a better future for his family. Esmeralda earned an Associate in Business Administration from Berkeley College in NJ as well as a Bachelor in Psychology from Rutger's University in NJ. Esmeralda lives in New Jersey with her husband and her three daughters. She currently homeschools her daughters ages 4, 10, and 12. In addition, she teaches CCD classes at her parish. She runs retreats on Powerful Prayers and leads a prayer group for a healing ministry. She is also the founder along with her husband, Brian of a pro-life movement that prays the Holy Rosary for the end of abortion. The movement is called, "The End of Abortion Movement: The Rosary is the Key." She is also the founder of "The House of Divino Nino" a website that promotes devotion to the Infancy of Jesus. The purpose of her writing is to help others get close to God, and to inspire her readers to seek God first above all things, to love God every day more and more and to motivate them to save their souls as well as their neighbor's soul through Jesus for the Glory of God.

For more information or questions regarding the Adoption Movement go to: **theadoptionmovement.com**

Please join me in this great battle to save souls through Jesus Christ!

St Therese as St. Joan of Arc
St. Therese & St. Joan of Arc pray for us!

Group s →

<u>Adopted:</u>

Rinaldi Precision Machine
Corporation. (Adriana & husband)
          small business

Son John & Noelle

Padre Pio Group

John Lillis's fb

Lifeboat Coffee

Victims of Ebola &
          other plagues

All animals living outdoors,
such as pets like dogs & cats

CPSIA information can be obtained at www.ICGtesting.com
Printed in the USA
LVOW05s2255280314

379374LV00003B/210/P